DA~~TE DUE~~

621.8
ROY
C.1

Royston, Angela
Ramps and wedges

$28.21
BC#34880000024401

DATE DUE	BORROWER'S NAME
2-19-08	Loven Brown
2-27-08	Jazman Martin

621.8   BC#34880000024401 $28.21
ROY   Royston, Angela
             Ramps and wedges

RAMPS AND WEDGES

ANGELA ROYSTON

Heinemann Library
Chicago, Illinois

© 2001 Heinemann Library
a division of Reed Elsevier Inc.
Chicago, Illinois

Customer Service 888-454-2279
Visit our website at www.heinemannlibrary.com

Designed by Visual Image
Illustrations by Barry Atkinson
Originated by Dot Gradations
Printed in China

05 04 03
10 9 8 7 6 5 4 3 2

Library of Congress Cataloging-in-Publication Data
Royston, Angela.
      Ramps and Wedges / Angela Royston.
            p. cm. – (Machines in action)
      Includes bibliographical references and index.
      ISBN 1-57572-321-2 (HC), 1-4034-4086-7 (Pbk.)
      1. Simple Machines—Juvenile literature. 2. Inclined planes—Juvenile literature. 3. Wedges—Juvenile literature. [1. Inclined planes. 2. Wedges.] I. Title. II. Series.

TJ147 .R69 2000
621.8'11—dc21

00-029594

Acknowledgments
The author and publishers are grateful to the following for permission to reproduce copyright material: Cephas / Mick Rock, p. 4; Corbis / Kevin Fleming, p. 7; Photodisk, p. 24; Heinemann / Trevor Clifford, pp. 12, 17, 18, 19, 20, 21, 28, 29; John Walmsley, p.16; Robert Harding Picture Library / Peter Langone , p. 6; Sue Cunningham Photographic, p. 15; Sylvia Corday Photo Library / Humphrey Evans, p. 23; Telegraph Colour Library / Robert Clare, p. 5; F. McKinney, p. 10; Scott Markewitz, p. 11; Tony Stone Images / Chris Speedle, p. 13.

Cover photograph reproduced with permission of Science Photo Library.

Every effort has been made to contact copyright holders of any material reproduced in this book. Any omissions will be rectified in subsequent printings if notice is given to the publisher.

Some words are shown in bold, **like this.** You can find out what they mean by looking in the glossary.

CONTENTS

What Is a Ramp?

A ramp is a smooth slope, but it is also a simple machine. It does not look like a machine—it has no wires, levers, or handles. Levers, springs, screws, pulleys, and wheels are also simple machines.

It is easier to roll a barrel up a long gentle slope, or ramp, than up a steep slope.

A machine helps you to do work more easily. It is easier to walk up a long sloping ramp, even if it is farther, than it is to climb up a steep slope. And it takes less **force** to pull a heavy weight up a ramp than it does to lift the same weight straight up.

Try this!

Test a ramp. Make a slope with a board. Tie a piece of string around a heavy dictionary. Use one finger to test which is easier: pulling the dictionary up the slope, or lifting it straight up.

Many big buildings have a short flight of stairs up to the front door. People in wheelchairs can only get in and out of the front door if there is a ramp.

Wheels and ramps

A wheel is a simple machine that makes moving things easier. But you cannot wheel something up a flight of stairs. Multi-story parking garages use ramps so cars can drive from one level to another. Most public buildings, such as libraries and office buildings, have ramps for people in wheelchairs. This book shows how ramps work and how ramps are used.

Slopes and Slides

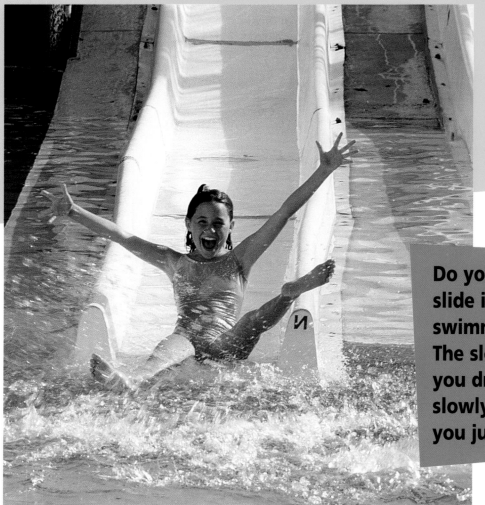

Do you like to slide into a swimming pool? The slope lets you drop more slowly than if you jumped in.

Slopes and ramps also make going down easier too. When you slip down the slide in the park, you travel a longer distance than you did climbing up the steps.

What can you do to make yourself slide more slowly? One way is to push your arms or legs against the side of the slide. The more you rub against the slide the more it slows you down. The rubbing is called **friction**.

Many big buildings have a short flight of stairs up to the front door. People in wheelchairs can only get in and out of the front door if there is a ramp.

Wheels and ramps

A wheel is a simple machine that makes moving things easier. But you cannot wheel something up a flight of stairs. Multi-story parking garages use ramps so cars can drive from one level to another. Most public buildings, such as libraries and office buildings, have ramps for people in wheelchairs. This book shows how ramps work and how ramps are used.

Slopes and Slides

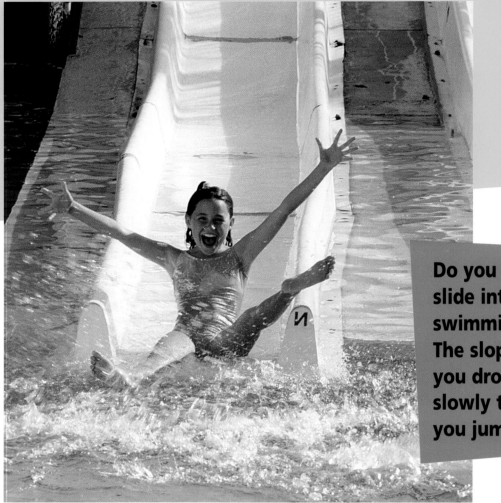

Slopes and ramps also make going down easier too. When you slip down the slide in the park, you travel a longer distance than you did climbing up the steps.

What can you do to make yourself slide more slowly? One way is to push your arms or legs against the side of the slide. The more you rub against the slide the more it slows you down. The rubbing is called **friction**.

Jump slides

Water skiers and snow skiers use ramps to jump into the air. The skier slides up the ramp so fast, she keeps moving after she has left the ramp. The ramp lifts her upward and forward. Some skiers jump high enough that they can perform acrobatic twists and somersaults in the air before they land.

This water skier is using a ramp to jump high above the water. Expert water skiers can jump as far as half the length of a soccer field.

Think about it!

When you use a slide to go into the swimming pool, do you go faster if you sit up or if you lean back? What do you think makes the difference?

Building the Pyramids

A ramp like this would have been three times as big as the pyramid.

The ramp was one of the earliest simple machines to be invented. The Ancient Egyptians built huge **pyramids** made of very large blocks of stones. The stone blocks were lifted into place without the help of trains, cranes, or even horses.

Archaeologists think that people-power alone, using just a few ramps and **rollers**, lifted the stones. It does not seem likely that one long ramp was used. Instead, the ramp was probably built around the pyramid, joining one level to the next, like the ramp in a multi-story parking garage.

8

Think about it!

Do you think the Egyptians made their ramps from mud or sand? What would have been the advantages and disadvantages of sand? If you were building a ramp to construct a huge stone pyramid, what material would you use for your ramp?

Pallets and rollers

The Ancient Egyptians used other simple machines. They used levers to move each block onto a **pallet.** Archaeologists think they might have used tree trunks as rollers to make it easier to pull the pallets.

The Egyptians used gangs of enslaved people to build the pyramids. Thousands of men probably worked for 20 years to finish the job.

Zigzag Journeys

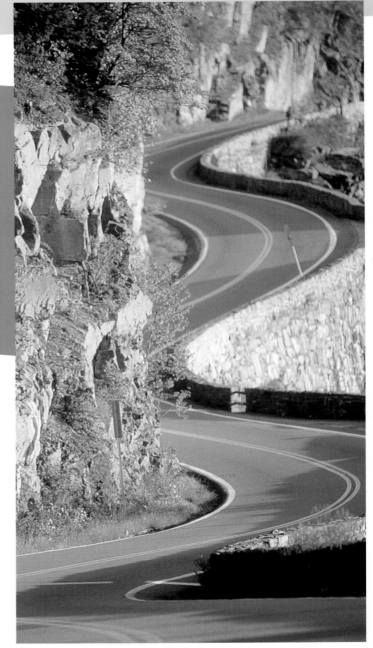

Many mountain roads make climbing easier by using a zigzag path. The zigzag spreads the climbing out over a longer distance.

It is hard work climbing straight up a steep mountain slope. Following a **zigzag** path makes the distance of the climb longer, but less steep.

Most cars cannot climb very steep hills. Engineers build mountain roads that zigzag up the slope. This makes the road easier and safer to drive up and down. The bends at the ends of each zigzag are sometimes very tight. The road almost turns in a full circle.

10

Make it work!

Draw a zigzag path from the top to the bottom of a sheet of paper. Measure how long it is. Now draw a straight line from the top to the bottom of the page and measure it. How much longer is the zigzag path than the straight path?

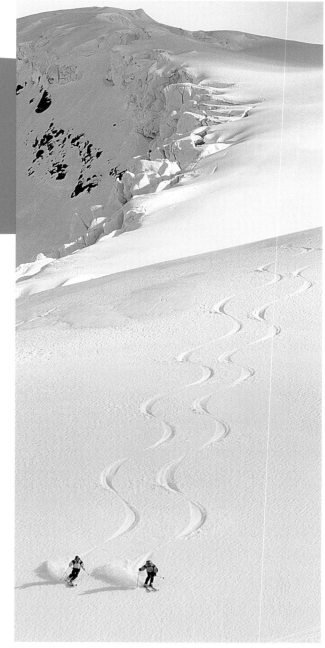

There is little friction between the skis and the snow so a skier can move very fast, even when he or she takes a zigzag path.

Skiing downhill

A zigzag path makes going downhill easier too. Skiers often zigzag down steep snow slopes. It helps them control their speed and come down more slowly. If they skied straight down a steep slope, they might lose control and fall.

What Is a Wedge?

The wedge pushes the door back and up so that it will stay open.

A **wedge** is a small ramp that stops heavy things from moving. For example, if you place a small, narrow wedge under a door, it will hold the door open. The thin edge of the wedge fits easily under the door, but as you try to close it, the door moves up the slope until it jams.

As the door pushes against the wedge, it increases the amount of **friction** between the wedge and the floor and stops the wedge from slipping. The rougher the floor, the better the wedge will work. A carpet will produce more friction than a smooth vinyl floor.

Try this!

Use different shaped objects, such as a book, a wedge, a box, and a ball, to jam a door. Which object works the best? Do heavier objects work better than light objects? Do any of the objects not work at all? Why do you think that is? Is it better to put the wedge at the hinge end or the doorknob end of the bottom of the door?

Starting blocks

In a race, **sprinters** use wedge-shaped blocks to push them off to a fast start. As the sprinters push their feet down and back, the angle of the blocks pushes them up and forward.

The slope of the starting block pushes the sprinter up and forward.

Powerful Wedges

The thin edge of the wedge is pushed under the weight. As the wedge is pushed farther and farther underneath, the weight lifts up little by little.

A small **wedge** can be used to lift a heavy weight. It takes less **force** than lifting the weight straight up because the tip of the wedge moves a long way to lift the weight just a little. The wedge changes the direction of the force—as the wedge is pushed forward, it lifts the weight up. Wedges are often used to lift a heavy weight just enough to get a lever underneath it.

Splitting a stone

Wedges are used to split chunks of stone, but the wedges cannot be used on their own. Instead, the stonecutter hits the thick end of the wedge with a heavy hammer. The thin edge cracks the stone. He hits in

The force of the hammer hitting the wide end of the wedge becomes an even stronger force at the sharp end.

another wedge next to it to make the crack larger. As he hits first one wedge and then the other, the wedges are forced into the crack, making it deeper. Eventually the stone splits in two.

Sharp Wedges

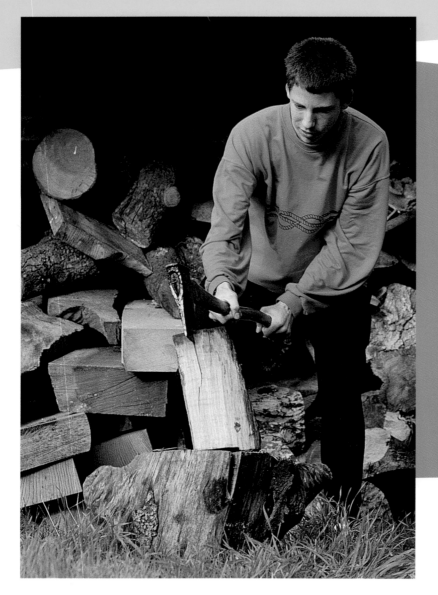

The woodcutter lifts the heavy head of the axe and lets it fall onto the log. All the weight of the fall is concentrated on the sharp edge of the blade. Axes are very sharp and dangerous, and should only be used by adults.

The **blade** of the axe is a thin, sharp **wedge**. As the blade hits the wood, all the **force** is concentrated on the sharp edge of the blade. Bit by bit the blade is pushed into the wood. As the thin edge of the blade moves in, the thicker end of the blade makes the split in the wood wider. Eventually the block of wood breaks into two parts.

Even a blunt knife will easily cut into an apple. The force on the handle is concentrated on the edge of the blade.

Knives

The blade of a knife is a wedge too. As you move the knife back and forth, the blade cuts into the apple. As the sharp edge of the blade moves down, the thicker part of the blade pushes the sides of the cut apart. Always have an adult nearby when you use a sharp knife.

Think about it!

The first axes were made of sharp pieces of hard, strong stone such as flint. Early people used one stone to chip the edge of a piece of flint to give it a sharp blade. The wedge-shaped flint was then tied to a wooden handle to make an axe.

Saws

A saw is a long knife with a **serrated**, or **zigzag**, **blade**. Some kitchen knives have a serrated edge too. They are particularly useful for cutting fruit and vegetables. The whole blade is **wedge**-shaped, like an ordinary knife, and the blade itself is split into many smaller wedges.

Different parts of the blade point in different directions. The sharp points dig into the wood and the sloping edges widen the cuts as the blade moves back and forth. The sharp edge on a serrated blade is longer than the sharp edge on an ordinary blade.

18

Hedge trimmer

The **hedge trimmer** has many wedge-shaped blades that move from side to side. As gaps open up between the blades, the stems of the bushes are caught between them. As the blades move across each other, they slice the stems.

An electric trimmer has two serrated blades that cut through twigs and thin branches easily.

Think about it!

Danger! Saws, knives, and axes are very sharp and can be dangerous. Be careful with knives, and keep a safe distance away from anyone using an axe or a saw. Electric knives, trimmers, and cutters are fast and powerful. Only adults should use them.

Scissors and Cutters

Scissors have two **wedge**-shaped **blades** that work together. When you open the scissors, the blades make a "V" shape. The blades trap the edge of the paper in the point of the "V" and cut from both sides. As you close the handles, the blades **force** the paper apart.

Different shaped scissors are used to cut different things.

Scissors produce a strong force at the point where they cut, and the long blades allow you to control the cut. You can cut a straight edge, or you can cut around a wavy line.

20

Pruning shears have very sharp blades to cut through the tough woody stems on bushes and shrubs.

Pruning Shears

Pruning shears are used in the garden. They cut through twigs and thin branches. They have short, curved blades and handles for the gardener to hold. The handles move a long way to come together, and the blades move a short way to come together. This produces a strong cutting force between the blades.

Spades, Jackhammers, and Plows

A spade is one of the simplest digging tools. Jackhammers use motors and specially shaped blades to break up different kinds of ground.

Gardeners use a spade with a **wedge**-shaped **blade** and a long handle to dig into the soil. The gardener often puts a foot on top of the blade and uses his or her weight to push the blade into the soil with more force. The long handle is a lever which makes it easier to lift the chunk of soil and turn it over.

Think about it!

Gardeners use trowels, hoes, and pitchforks to do different jobs in the garden. Find out what each is used for. How does the shape of each make it particularly suited to the job it does?

A plow has sharp, curved blades. The sharp edge of each blade cuts into the soil, and the curve turns the soil over.

Mechanical diggers

A jackhammer is used to break up the surface of the road. It has a narrow wedge-shaped blade. The motor makes the blade hit the road with many short, sharp bangs.

Some mechanical diggers, like bulldozers and plows, are much bigger than jackhammers. A bulldozer has a long sharp blade for cutting into the earth. A plow has many curved blades.

The Incredible Zipper

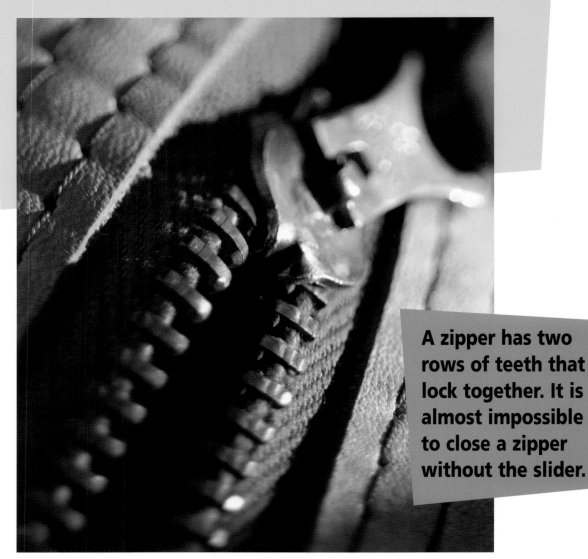

A zipper has two rows of teeth that lock together. It is almost impossible to close a zipper without the slider.

A zipper is a quick and easy way to fasten a coat, but it was only invented just over a hundred years ago. At that time women wore long boots that were fastened with laces hooked around lots of tiny buttons. The zipper was invented as an easier way to fasten boots. Zippers are now used to fasten jeans, jackets, cushion covers, bags, and many other things. What else do you have that fastens with a zipper?

How a zipper works

A zipper has two rows of teeth that fit together to make a tight seam. The teeth are pushed together and pulled apart by a slider. The slider itself is **wedge**-shaped and inside the slider are three more wedges. When you pull the slider down, a wedge at the top pushes the teeth apart. When you pull the slider up, two wedges at the side push the teeth together.

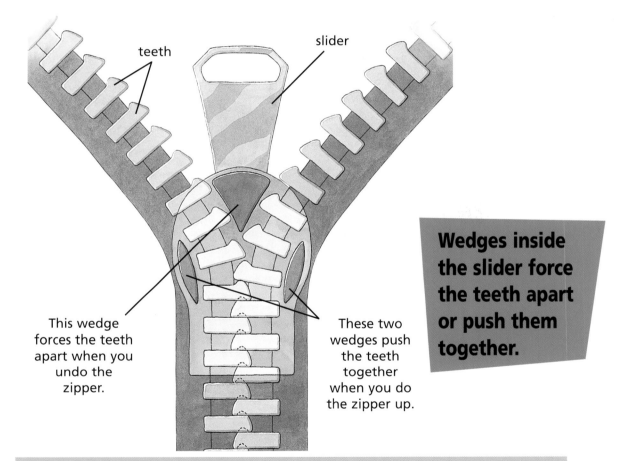

teeth

slider

This wedge forces the teeth apart when you undo the zipper.

These two wedges push the teeth together when you do the zipper up.

Wedges inside the slider force the teeth apart or push them together.

Think about it!

Why do you think most shoes use laces or velcro instead of zippers? What are the advantages of using zippers instead of buttons on clothes?

Lock and Key

pins stop barrel turning

springs to push pins down

split in pin

barrel of lock

Locked Door
While the splits in the pins are not lined up, the lock cannot be turned.

Does your front door have a lock with a notched metal key? This kind of lock is often called a Yale lock, after its inventor, Linus Yale. The key is a series of **wedges** which lift five pins inside the lock.

The lock consists of a round barrel in a metal block and five **split pins**. When the door is locked the pins hold the barrel in the lock. The lock can only be turned when the splits in the pins line up along the gap between the barrel and the block.

Opening the lock

Each pin is split at a different height. When you put the notched key into the lock, the notches wedge each pin up so the splits line up. Then the key can be turned to open the door. Each lock has a different combination of split pins, so only the right key will open it. Each notch is roughly "V" shaped. This allows the key to slide in and out of the lock.

key

splits line up

key and barrel turns

Unlocked Door
When the splits in the pins line up, the key can turn.

Make it work!

Draw a design for a Yale lock and key. Remember you have to split each pair of pins in a different place. Then you have to draw notches on the key that will make the splits line up. Make sure your key is able to slip in and out of the lock.

Make a Zigzag Bottle Run

Use empty plastic bottles and cardboard tubes to make a ramp for rolling balls or marbles down.

You will need:

- a flight of stairs with a banister
- 6–12 large empty plastic bottles or cardboard tubes
- scissors
- string
- small balls (such as ping-pong balls) or large marbles

1 Ask an adult to cut a slice off the bottom and top of each bottle.

2 Ask an adult to cut a bite out of one end of each bottle and cardboard tube.

3 Tie the first bottle to the banister at the top of the stairs. Tie it at an angle so that it slopes down.

4 Position the second bottle so that the hole in the top is underneath the end of the bottle above. Tie the second bottle to the banisters so that it slopes downward and backward.

5 Carry on with the next bottle pointing forwards and then the next one downward or backward, and so on until you have used all the bottles and tubes.

6 Drop a ball into the bottle at the top of the stairs and watch it travel all the way down.

7 Try running model cars down the bottle run. You may have to change the run to make the bottles slope less steeply.

Glossary

blade sharp, flat cutting part of a knife or other instrument

force push or pull that makes something move

friction rubbing between two surfaces as one slides over the other

hedge trimmer tool with many sharp blades used to cut hedges

pruning shears tool with two short, sharp blades for cutting twigs

pallet platform heavy loads are put on to move them

pyramid three-dimensional shape with a square base and triangular sides

roller cylinder that rolls

serrated having a sharp, zigzag edge

split pin pin which is cut into two parts

sprinter athlete who runs fast races over a short distance

wedge triangular-shaped block

zigzag jagged with many sharp turns from one side to the other

Answers to Questions

p. 7 You slide faster if you lie back. When you lie back, your body is more streamlined. Although more of your body touches the slide, the water reduces the friction between the two surfaces. When you sit up, the air catches your body and slows you down. Also, your weight presses on a smaller area of the slide and increases the friction.

p. 9 Egyptians probably used earth or mud to build their ramps. Plenty of sand would have been available since the pyramids are built on the edge of the desert, but the pallets and rollers would have sunk into the sand.

p. 13 Heavier objects make better wedges than lighter objects of the same shape, but even small, light wedges can work. Balls do not make good wedges because there is little friction with the floor, and they roll too easily. It is best to put a wedge at the doorknob end of the door.

p. 15 When you fold paper several times, the folds are thicker than the loose edges. So it is better to put the loose edges under the leg.

p. 21 It should be easier to control the scissors if you hold them steady and move the paper.

p. 23 A trowel is small with high sides for scooping up small amounts of earth. A hoe has a flat, horizontal blade and a long handle for digging up weeds without having to bend over. A pitchfork has pointed prongs to make it easier to dig into heavy or hard earth.

p. 25 Shoes use laces or velcro so that they will fit a wider range of feet. You can tie laces tighter if your foot is narrow or leave the laces loose if your foot is wide. A zipper, however, cannot be adjusted. Zippers on clothes are quicker to do and undo than buttons.

Index

More Books to Read

Dahl, Michael. *Inclined Planes.* Danbury, Conn.: Children's Press, 1996.

Lafferty, Peter. *What's Inside Everyday Things?* Lincolnwood, Ill: N.T.C. Contemporary Publishing Co., 1995.

Whittle, Fran. *Simple Machines.* Austin, Tex.: Raintree Steck-Vaughn Publishers, 1997.